WEAPONIZING POOP

Jeff Mapua

Enslow Publishing
101 W. 23rd Street
Suite 240
New York, NY 10011
USA
enslow.com

Words to Know

artillery shell What a large weapon, such as a rocket or cannon, fires or throws forward.

bacteria Tiny single-celled organisms that cause diseases in plants and animals.

expose To leave without protection.

fertilizer Something to help soil produce larger or more plant life.

import To bring goods in from another country.

infect To cause a disease or illness.

malodorant A chemical that smells so bad that it temporarily stuns a person.

predator An animal that lives by killing and eating other animals.

virus Simple microorganism or very complicated molecule that causes diseases in plants and animals.

Contents

Animal Kingdom

All animals poop. It is a basic fact of life. But not all animals treat poop in the same way. A lot of animals stay away from their own poop. They do this to keep themselves clean. For example, birds drop their poop from the sky to keep it far away from their bodies. Some animals do something much different. They turn their poop into a weapon!

Some types of caterpillars get rid of their waste by firing it away at a distance up to 40 times their body length. This is the same as a 6-foot-tall person flinging their poop 240 feet away. The caterpillar poop comes out in a pellet and travels about 4.2 feet per second. Scientists found

FUN FACT

One insect uses its poop to protect itself. Young tortoise beetles, called larvae, pile up poop on their backs to make a shield. This helps keep predators from eating them.

The orb weaver spider's web and markings make it look like bird poop, so the birds don't eat it!

that caterpillars do this to protect themselves from predators, such as wasps.

The orb weaver spider uses poop as a way to keep predators away, too. It does not use its own poop. Instead, it pretends to be bird poop. The spider spins a special shape into its web. When it sits on the shape, it looks like bird poop!

Poop in the Past

People use poop as a weapon, too. In fact, people have been using poop as a weapon for thousands of years. Around the year 400 BCE, archers were known to use poop on their arrows. In the area now known as the Ukraine and Russia, there were a group of people called the Scythians. The Scythians dipped their arrows in feces and dead bodies. The arrows would cause gangrene, a disease where flesh and tissue die because of an infection. They would also cause tetanus, an infection that causes painful muscle spasms and death. These poison arrows made it extra

Art from around 570 BCE shows a Scythian archer who used hemlock poison in addition to contaminated arrows.

deadly for anyone hit by one. It was said the arrows smelled so bad that people did not have to be hit by one to suffer!

The ancient Romans had a similar idea. They would spread manure and the flesh of dead animals on their swords. Just like the poison arrows, these poisoned swords were extra dangerous for anyone cut by one.

A catapult is a machine that launches an object great distances. They were used in ancient warfare, and the Chinese added their own twist to the weapon. In the twelfth century, they would make a "bomb" out of gunpowder, poison, and human poop. This giant ball was held together with hemp string. They loaded the catapult with this smelly weapon and lit the "bomb" with a hot poker. With the poop and gunpowder lit, the Chinese would fling the ball at their enemies.

The ancient Chinese also invented a smaller catapult that was very accurate.

Poop in the Past, Part Two

In the 1940s, the United States invented a weapon that really stunk. Although it used no poop, it sprayed a chemical on its targets that made them smell like they had a bathroom accident. The weapon, called Who Me, was top secret. There are no known records of it ever being used, and it ended up being unsuccessful.

One story from the 1950s shows how creative people can be. The Canadian government tried to force Inuit families to move to another part of the country. One elder man refused to go. His family could not convince him to move, so they left him in an igloo without his tools.

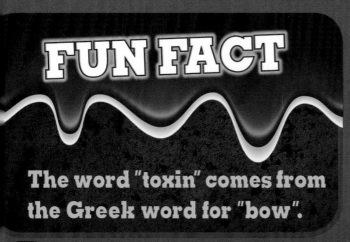

FUN FACT

The word "toxin" comes from the Greek word for "bow".

They thought he would eventually change his mind. Instead, the elder Inuit froze his poop and shaped it like a knife. He used this poop knife to kill an animal. He used the body to make a sled and escaped the government.

In the 1960s, during the Vietnam War, poop was again used as a weapon. The Vietnamese fighters invented a weapon called punji sticks. These sticks were made from bamboo that was sharpened. The sticks were then dipped in human poop and poison from plants and animals. They would hide the spears in the ground or under a trapdoor. Like the arrows used centuries earlier, the spears could cause infections and even death.

Soldiers in Vietnam who were injured by punji sticks had to be taken to safety by helicopter.

Bat and Bird Boom

Bird and bat poop is called guano. Guano is a good source of different chemicals. These include ammonia, uric acid, phosphorus, nitrates, and more. In the nineteenth century, Europeans discovered that guano was also an excellent source of saltpeter. Saltpeter is potassium and sodium nitrate. It is used in fertilizer and explosives. However, it cannot be used to make a bomb because the amount needed would be impractical.

After Europeans discovered the secret of guano, bird and bat poop suddenly became very valuable. Historians say that when large amounts of guano were discovered, it even helped increase the number of people on Earth!

FUN FACT

In the 1980s, the United States accused the Soviet Union of using a biochemical weapon. They called it "yellow rain". The United States believed that the yellow clouds were poisonous. However, "yellow rain" turned out to be showers of poop from Southeast Asian Honeybees.

Guano, shown here with an insect wing, was once a very valuable substance.

The best guano was considered to come from Peru and Chile in South America. Countries fought over the valuable guano in what is known as the Guano Wars of 1865–66. The United States even claimed unnamed and uninhabited islands if they had guano.

Guano Gunpowder

Guano was used to make fertilizer and explosives in the 1800s, but people found another use for bird and bat poop. Guano is made of potassium nitrate, or saltpeter, which can be used to make gunpowder. It takes one hundred pounds of bat droppings to make just four pounds of saltpeter.

During the time when people were fighting over guano, war broke out in the United States. This came to be known as the American Civil War that took place from 1861 to 1865. Guano then became an important resource for Americans. Unlike other countries, the United States did not need to import guano. The United States had its own

FUN FACT

A man in Arizona found a new use for rabbit poop. He invented a flamethrower that uses rabbit poop as fuel. The fuel is made by grinding the rabbit poop into a fine powder. He also makes methane by letting the rabbit poop chemically react with water.

The Battle of Pea Ridge during the Civil War may have featured guano gunpowder.

caves filled with guano in the southeastern part of the country. These bat caves were known as "peter caves."

During the Civil War, the South, or Confederate army, mined these peter caves. Not only did the guano have the chemical ingredients for gunpowder, but the ground did, too. At one cave in Arkansas, the Confederate army built fourteen buildings in 1862 as part of a guano-mining operation. They mined the guano until January 1863, when the North, or Union army, captured and destroyed it.

Stink Bombs and More

The use of poop in warfare started centuries ago, and it continues through today. At the University of Florida, researchers are looking into a way to turn poop into rocket fuel. Their idea is to use a special type of bacteria that turns organic materials, such as poop, food, and paper, into methane. In their experiments, one person was able to make seventy-seven gallons of methane fuel per week!

The United States Army had a new secret weapon in 2008 called the XM1063. How the weapon works is classified information. However, based on the description of what it does, it could be called a "stink bomb."

The weapon fires a nonlethal projectile that scatters 152 smaller parts. Each of these 152 parts parachutes down from the sky while spraying a chemical around. Since the weapon is classified,

The M198 howitzer, shown here, is used to fire rockets at targets.

few people know exactly what the weapon sprays. Many believe that the chemical is a malodorant. A malodorant is a chemical that smells so bad that it temporarily stuns a person. The weapon is used to impair enemies without killing or harming them permanently.

In Russia, a man created a way to fire poop from a tank. Soldiers combine their waste with explosives in an artillery shell. This method also solved the problem of removing soldiers' waste from inside the tank. The inventor intends to damage enemies emotionally as well as physically.

These Russian tanks fire regular ammunition, unlike the poop tank.

Tiny Terrors

How did dipping arrows in feces make them poisonous? The reason poop can be used as a weapon in this way is because of little organisms and cells that live in it. These are called bacteria and viruses.

Poop can carry different types of harmful bacteria and viruses. Some bacteria and viruses grow inside the digestive system of animals. When an infected animal poops, the bacteria or virus can be found in the animal's waste. Touching the feces can transfer the bacteria or virus.

Bacteria are tiny single-celled organisms. They live in large numbers in almost every

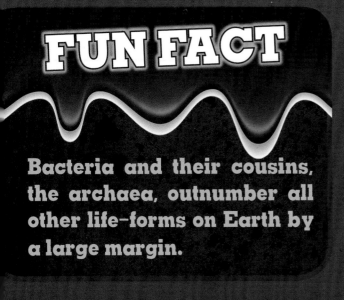

FUN FACT

Bacteria and their cousins, the archaea, outnumber all other life-forms on Earth by a large margin.

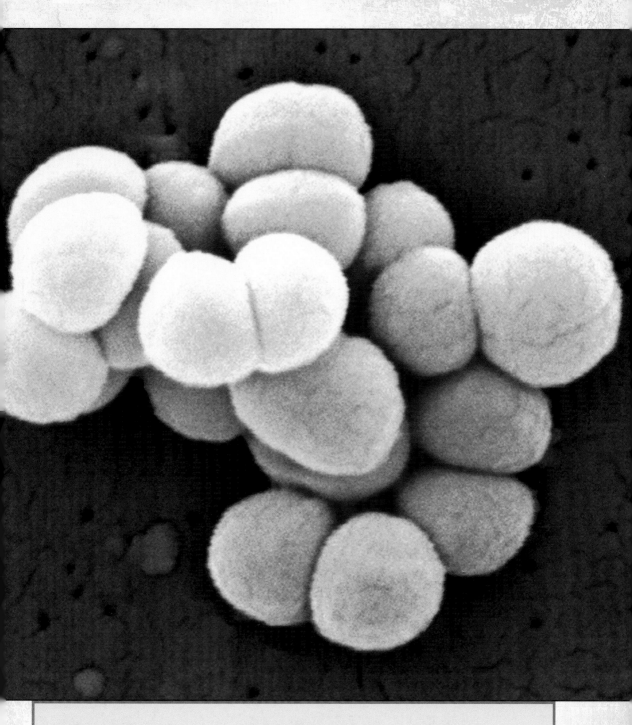

Micrococcus luteus is a bacteria often found inside a person's mouth.

environment on Earth. Bacteria are small and are of a simple design. They can grow and divide very quickly. There are many different kinds of bacteria. A good number of them can cause diseases and illness in people. Some types of bacteria produce toxins that are harmful to people. Other bacteria multiply so quickly that they overwhelm a body.

By definition, a virus is not an organism or life-form. It cannot make copies of itself without help from another life-form, such as animals, plants, or bacteria. A virus is a parasite. Viruses infect other organisms to make copies of themselves. They are small and simple. Their name means "slimy liquid" or "poison" in Latin. A virus can be very harmful to people. Some viruses attack a person's nervous system. This causes illness.

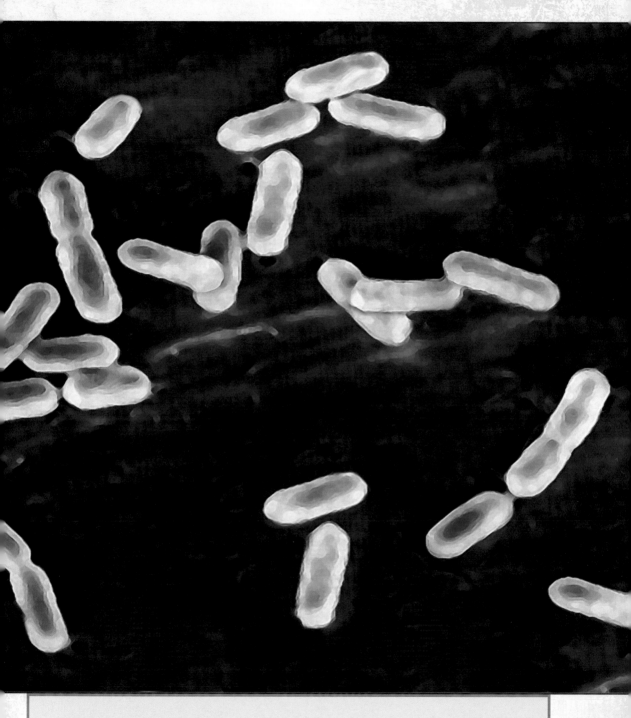

Listeria monocytogenes is a bacteria that can cause flu-like symptoms in people.

Poop Poison

People are sometimes exposed to poop from different animals. This can happen while walking outside or interacting with a pet. The Illinois Poison Center said that most exposures are not dangerous to a person's health. However, exposure to many different types of feces can still be dangerous. It is helpful to understand what in poop can cause a person harm and the symptoms these organisms can produce.

FUN FACT

What is in a name? There are many different names for poop. These include feces, waste, scat, number two, stool, dung, doo-doo, caca, excrement, and many more.

Cleaning up dog poop helps people avoid dangerous bacteria and viruses.

Many people have dogs or encounter dogs in their everyday life. With the number of dogs around, it is not surprising to accidentally touch or step in their poop. But just stepping on dog waste is not dangerous. A person would have to accidentally ingest it for it to be dangerous. If that feces is infected with a bacteria called *Campylobacter*, it can cause nausea, vomiting, stomach pain, cramping, diarrhea, and fever.

Ingestion is also the main way human feces can cause fatigue, nausea, loss of appetite, diarrhea, vomiting, and fever. Human feces is dangerous when it is infected with the hepatitis A virus.

Cat poop can sometimes be infected with a parasite called *Toxoplasma gondii*. If a person were to ingest infected cat feces, it could cause flu-like symptoms, confusion, and seizures. It is particularly dangerous for pregnant women because it can pass on to the baby.

Cat poop should be handled carefully to keep dangerous parasites away.

Living Weapons

Weaponizing poop is a way to take advantage of the bacteria and viruses it carries. However, people have discovered that they do not need poop to weaponize bacteria and viruses. They can make biological weapons out of these tiny organisms and parasites.

Biological warfare is the use of disease-causing bacteria and viruses as a weapon against an enemy. The Scythian archers in 400 BCE and the fighters in the Vietnam War, with their poop-covered punji sticks, used biological weapons.

Biological weapons work by infecting a target with an agent that causes illness or even death. The target can be people, but it can also be animals or food crops. The weapons work based

FUN FACT

There have been accounts of people injecting feces into a victim. It can cause fever, illness, and death.

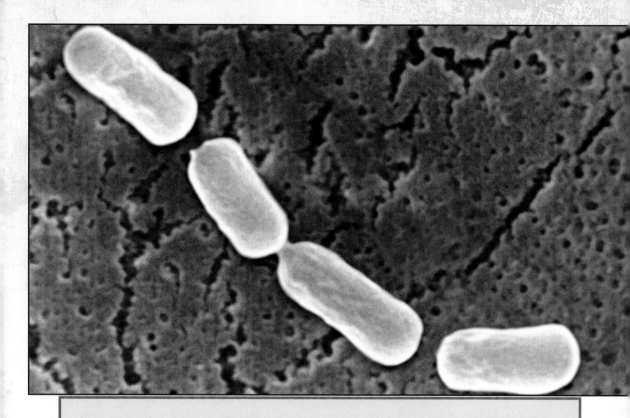

Clostridium botulinum bacteria grow on food and can cause paralysis and even death.

on how the bacteria or viruses need to get into a target's body.

For example, the bacteria *Clostridium botulinum* causes the deadly condition botulism. Usually this bacteria infects people through food. But it can also be inhaled. Weapons can be made to spray targets with an agent that causes botulism. Many other biological weapons are based on agents

Porcupine puffer fish can expand into a ball by inflating their bodies, which are covered with poisonous spines.

that are inhaled. Saxitoxin, the poison found in Japanese puffer fish, is fired from rifles.

Biological weapons are mostly inhaled, infect open wounds, or contaminate food and water. There are thousands of toxins that occur in nature. However, only about 160 of these can be used to harm people. Of these 160, only 30 are considered usable as biological weapons.

Learn More

Books

Baby Professor. *Germs, Fungus, and Other Stuff That Makes Us Sick*. Newark, DE: Speedy Publishing, 2015.

Baum, Margaux, and Amy Romano. *Germ Warfare*. New York, NY: Rosen Publishing Group, 2017.

Koontz, Robin Michal. *Poop Is Power!* Vero Beach, FL: Rourke Educational Media, 2016.

McGuinness, Janelle. *Secret School: Spy Squad*. NSW, Australia: Techiworx, 2016

Websites

Easy Science for Kids, "Excretory System Basics"
easyscienceforkids.com/the-scoop-on-poop-human-excretory-system-basics/
How does your body make poop?

Kids Health, "What Are Germs?"
http://kidshealth.org/en/kids/germs.html
Learn about germs and viruses.

National Geographic Kids, "8 Awesome Things Living on You"
http://kids.nationalgeographic.com/explore/awesome-8-hub/things-on-you/
The amazing things that live in, on, and with you every day.

Index

Published in 2018 by Enslow Publishing, LLC.
101 W. 23rd Street, Suite 240, New York, NY 10011

Copyright © 2018 by Enslow Publishing, LLC.
All rights reserved.

Library of Congress Cataloging-in-Publication Data

Names: Mapua, Jeff.
Title: Weaponizing poop / Jeff Mapua.
Description: New York : Enslow Publishing, [2018] | Series:
The power of poop | Audience: Grades 3-5. | Includes
bibliographical references and index.
Identifiers: LCCN 2017021995| ISBN 9780766090958 (library
bound) | ISBN 9780766090934 (pbk.) | ISBN 9780766090941
(6 pack) Subjects: LCSH: Biological warfare—Miscellanea—
Juvenile literature. | Feces—Miscellanea—Juvenile literature. |
Military weapons—Miscellanea—Juvenile literature.
Classification: LCC UG447.8 .M315 2018 | DDC 623.4/594—
dc23
LC record available at https://lccn.loc.gov/2017021995

Printed in the United States of America

Photo Credits: Cover Sergey Kamshylin/Shutterstock.com;
p. 2 Vracovska/Shutterstock.com; p. 5 Arterra Picture
Library/Alamy Stock Photo; pp. 6–7 DEA/G. Dagli Orti
/De Agostini/Getty Images; pp. 8–9 Michael Nicholson
/Corbis Historical/Getty Images; p. 11 Bettmann
/Getty Images; p. 13 Chris Howes/Wild Places/Alamy Stock
Photo; p. 15 Buyenlarge/Archive Photos/Getty Images;
p. 17 Anwar Amro/AFP/Getty Images; pp. 18–19 Mikhail
Metzel/TASS/Getty Images; pp. 20–21, 22–23, 29 BSIP
/Universal Images Group/Getty Images; p. 25 W. Scott
McGill/Shutterstock.com; pp. 26–27 KARNSTOCKS/
Shutterstock.com; p. 30 Mr. James Kelley/Shutterstock.com;
back cover (background), interior pages inset boxes (bottom)
jessicahyde/Shutterstock.com; remaining interior pages
(background) Nik Merkulov/Shutterstock.com; interior pages
inset boxes (top) Reamolko/Shutterstock.com.